Doris Day and Kitschy Melodies

ALSO BY PHYLLIS KOESTENBAUM

Criminal Sonnets

Necessary Mistake

14 Criminal Sonnets

That Nakedness

Hunger Food

oh I can't she says

Crazy Face

PROSE POEMS

Doris Day and Kitschy Melodies

PHYLLIS KOESTENBAUM

—
—
·
—
—

La Questa
PRESS

La Questa Press
211 La Questa Way
Woodside, California 94062

www.laquestapress.com

ISBN 0-9644348-4-9

Library of Congress Control Number: 00-136389

Cover and text design by Kajun Design

Cover Art © Tony Arruza/Corbis

Author photo © Reid Yalom

PUBLICATIONS FROM LA QUESTA PRESS

Trouble No More by Anthony Grooms
The Wine of Astonishment by Mary Overton
Zombi, You My Love by William Orem

LA QUESTA PRESS POETRY SERIES

Earthlight by Hannah Stein
Doris Day and Kitschy Melodies by Phyllis Koestenbaum

Acknowledgments

I thank the editors of the following journals and anthologies in which poems, some with different titles and in earlier versions, previously appeared:

American Letters & Commentary: "Kings Highway Poet" (as "Ars Poetica"), "Stanley Elkin" (as "Xerox Machine")

Barnabe Mountain Review: "Anne or Ann" (as "His Finding My Friend with a Boston Accent Interesting")

Compact Bone: "Grace Kelly" (as "Cheesecake"), "Juliet" (as "Who Is She"), "Suicided Novelist" (as "Death, Comparison and Tandoori Chicken")

Epoch: "Alexander Pope" (as "Blind Alleys"), "Birthday Girl" (as "Two Scoops in Two Dishes"), "Glenn Gould" (as "My Friend with a Future in Art"), "Maria Callas on Broadway" (as "Flowering Destinies"), "Saint Joan" (as "The Library"), "Young Armless Man in the Barbecue Restaurant" (as "Admission of Failure")

Heresies: "Unavenging Japanese Father" (as "A TV Movie")

Poetry New York: "Harriet Feigenbaum Is a Sculptor," "Proust"

Quarter After Eight: "Mother Teresa" (as "Running from Hitler"), "Shirley" (as "Eye Device"), "Walt Whitman" (as "How to Win the War Effort")

Verse: Prose Poem Feature: "Miss Kramer" (as "Stealing from Your Daughter")

"Harriet Feigenbaum Is a Sculptor" was republished in *The Best American Poetry 1993* (Scribner) and *Telling Stories* (W.W. Norton).
"Ulysses" (as "40 Years Later") was published in *The Times of Our Lives: Women Writing on Sex after 40* (Crossing Press).
"Young Armless Man in the Barbecue Restaurant" (as "Admission of Failure") was republished in *Night Out: Poems about Hotels, Motels, Restaurants, and Bars* (Milkweed Editions); *Oral Interpretation* (Houghton Mifflin); and *The Best American Poetry 1992* (Scribner).

I also thank the Fine Arts Work Center in Provincetown for a Senior Fellowship and the Arts Council of Santa Clara County for an Artist Fellowship.

And I thank William Fry, Janice Heiss and Joyce James—

Kathy Barr, Edith Gelles and Donna Reese—

Rose Catacalos, Thaisa Frank, Carolyn Grassi, Audrey Hannah and Lynn Wardley.

For Aaron Goldman

———∞———

For Elissa Koestenbaum
Ian Koestenbaum
Joshua Koestenbaum
Wayne Koestenbaum

Doris Day and Kitschy Melodies

Contents

Young Armless Man and Others

3   Young Armless Man in the Barbecue Restaurant

4   Alban Berg

5   Kings Highway Poet

6   A Trim Young Extra

7   Maria Callas on Broadway

8   Prose Poet

9   My Sister-in-law Leatrice

10   A Strauss Heroine

11   Suicided Novelist

12   Lucia di Lammermoor

13   Ulysses

14   Princess Elizabeth

15   Morty's Ex-Wife

16   Proust

17   Shirley

18   Grace Kelly

19   Doris Lessing

20   Cassandra and Irene

Mussolini and Others

25   Mussolini et al.

26   André Gide

28   Samuel Beckett

29   Harriet Feigenbaum Is a Sculptor

30   Harry Levin's Shakespeare

31   Alexander Pope

33   Walt Whitman

34   Girl Boys Shoved Broomstick Up

35   Dr. J

36   Bette Davis

37   Disney

38 Greta Garbo in Queens

40 Tiny Tim

41 The Other Phyllis

43 Glenn Gould

45 Black Narcissus

46 Anne or Ann

47 Tall Deanna Durbin

48 Queen for a Day

Saint Joan and Others

53 Saint Joan

54 My Father's Half Brother Abe's Mother

55 Mother Teresa

56 Video Clerk with No Hand

58 Jewish Shakespeare

59 Hilda Doolittle and Other Modern American Poets

61 Tristan

62 Miss Kramer

63 Hemingway

65 Eunice

66 Blond Moviegoer

67 Joyce

69 Unavenging Japanese Father

70 Terese

71 Vietnam Son

72 Juliet

73 Rembrandt

74 Italian Rose

76 Stanley Elkin

78 Brooklyn Ballerina

79 Alan Roland

81 Birthday Girl

Young Armless Man and Others

————

————

————

————

————

Young Armless Man in the Barbecue Restaurant

The hostess seats a girl and a young man in a short-sleeve sport shirt with one arm missing below the shoulder. I'm at the next table with my husband and son, Andy's Barbecue Restaurant, an early evening in July, chewing a boneless rib eye, gulping a dark beer ordered from the cocktail waitress, a nervous woman almost over the hill, whose high heel sandals click back and forth from the bar to the dining room joined to the bar by an open arch. A tall heavy cook in white hat is brushing sauce on the chicken and spareribs rotating slowly on a squeaking spit. Baked potatoes heat on the oven floor. The young man is eating salad with his one hand. He and his girl are on a date. He has a forties' movie face, early Van Johnson before the motorcycle accident scarred his forehead. He lost the arm recently. Hard as it is, it could be worse. I would even exchange places with him if I could. *I want to exchange places with the young armless man in the barbecue restaurant.* He would sit at my table and I would sit at his. After dinner I would go in his car and he would go in mine. I would live in his house and work at his job and he would live in my house and do what I do. I would be him dressing and undressing and he would be me dressing and undressing. Our bill comes. My husband leaves the tip on the tray; we take toothpicks and mints and walk through the dark workingman's bar out to the parking lot still lit by the sky though the streetlights have come on as they do automatically at the same time each night. We drive our son, home for the summer, back to his job at the bookstore. As old Italians and Jews say of sons from five to fifty, he's a good boy. I have worked on this paragraph for more than two years.

Alban Berg

At first I thought the woman with Jane Bowles's haircut was Jane Bowles's biographer. I think I think people resemble others because in a new place I want to see people I know or at least recognize. The woman playing Schumann's "Scenes from Childhood" so beautifully was also very nice. A child's face on her and a sophisticated brightly and largely patterned dress. She explains repetition of themes and motifs in the entire piece. And looks like Louise, as if they were in the same family way back—did Louise's family come from Russia. Damn, but I missed the first scenes. We needed to bend under the low shrubs or rather the hanging tree—bend and lower the umbrella. Alban Berg songs on the radio. Variations of the same events week after week. The young women all sounding alike are planning a party—one says at a party she went to the one giving it typed up recipes and handed them like class assignments to guests to cook. I'm more interested in overheard conversations than in anything I'm saying or care to say. And two rows of conversation on-screen: the man talking to himself and repeating inessentials, in a rhythm, obsessively, I think a rhythm. A young woman strokes another woman's shoulder. Another woman strokes another woman's incredibly fine long hair, loose, with tiny braids, one or two. I'm never in my own head exclusively, except the other day when I allowed myself to break down. I will not say why—for the sake of not losing you, for the sake of this writing.

Kings Highway Poet

A Russian Jew knocks on a door in the suburbs to ask to be allowed to use the bathroom. The woman of the house says no. In her living room a beautiful young poet, whose star is rising, sleeps on a cot. She tries to bleed herself of ego, she wears her long wavy hair in a braid. My brother, a medical student, took me to his Brooklyn hospital and tested my blood. In our house, where I worried about dying, iron deficiency anemia was an acceptable illness, like measles or hay fever. When I was in high school and wrote poems, I took the bus to my school doctor for allergy shots. I was strongly attracted to this stout blond doctor and loved to receive allergy shots, even loved my arm's subsequent swelling and throbbing. One late Friday afternoon, after getting my weekly shot, riding home on the Kings Highway bus, the seats all taken so I was holding a strap for part of the 30-minute trip I always wished took longer, I looked at the other passengers going home or to the store or to visit someone they loved—you know how people on moving vehicles lose themselves. As if I'd never looked at them before, I could tell that these passengers staring at no one in particular were at home in the rightness of their simplest actions. This was psychological, not moral. In this order in this poem: a woman escaping persecution who needs to use the bathroom is not permitted to enter a house where a poet with long hair is sleeping on a cot in the living room; my brother took me to the hospital to test my blood but I was afraid of different diseases; I wrote poems in high school; I was given allergy shots. One Friday, riding home on the bus from the doctor I had a crush on, I realized that other people believed they were good.

A Trim Young Extra

I edited a manuscript. It was a lot of work, much more than the copy-editing I agreed to, and now the publisher won't pay the agreed rate. An agency got me the job and a man at the agency, who is not the friendly person who referred me to the publisher and whom I consulted during the early stages of the editing, wants me to compromise. My typist, who is my friend and a born underdog, wants me not to compromise. None of the cars parked in front of my townhouse complex is more than a couple of years old. A trim young woman in a royal blue striped shirt walks briskly by. I was attracted to this townhouse because of its many large windows. I had lived for 30 years in a house with overgrown trees and small windows which let in little if any sun. In this house my study is on the lowest of three levels and has two windows, one as high as the ceiling, the other slanted and higher (this will be hard to picture). These windows let in so much sun I had to have special blinds made to keep it out. The company that sold me the blinds (they weren't cheap) and installed them couldn't get them hung right. Eventually I compromised—they don't shut perfectly but they do the job.

Maria Callas on Broadway

Eventually the marriage of Daniel Barenboim and Jacqueline du Pré, ill with multiple sclerosis, puffed up from medication, fell apart. I'm not saying it could or should have been otherwise. We sat in the front row at her concert, my husband, not yet traveling to Europe with his young mistress, my teenage son, already a serious cellist, and I, before I'd started writing poems while my youngest child was at school, from 10 until 2 in the master bedroom at a small desk, the first I'd owned. Bruno Bettelheim's suicide—barely coterminus with my reawakened passion for poetry, I read Bruno Bettelheim and Isaac Bashevis Singer. When some fact about Singer's personal life disturbed me, sullied his image, I still read each new novel in hardcover, but less enthusiastically, although of course the work could have weakened. How bothered was I by Eliot's anti-Semitism. It never came up in Ciardi's class although Sacco and Vanzetti did. I also read Georges Simenon novels, novel after novel, and novels I'd read reviews of. *Manchild in the Promised Land.* I felt hopeful because of the talent of my children, their flowering destinies. Arturo Toscanini was conducting the NBC Symphony in Beethoven's 9th when, or after which, I left to babysit Martha and her little brother across the hall. Click click went the heels of dolled mothers as they walked to the elevator on Saturday nights. If my mother cried when my brother, at 16, left for Harvard, she did it behind her closed door—the apartment seemed even darker under the shroud of her exclusive loss. Patti LuPone played Maria Callas on Broadway: from nowhere comes Patti LuPone. Joan, a philosophy major, outwitted all of us gathered in the dorm living room after dates to talk and argue inconsequential points and subjects with passion. I'd suddenly leave the fray, peel off clothes like the past, like petals, as I rushed to my room, ready for bed the minute I got there.

Prose Poet

While I eat my canned chicken broth, which I swear resembles urine, I look out the window at my neighbor's blooming roses, one yellow, one red, buds last time I looked. My potted plants seem sloppy by comparison, white flowers that spot the deck like bird droppings. My friend, deprived of her small children, without a house or job, is concentrating on what she has inside. I also need to concentrate—four grown children, house with mortgage, two part-time jobs. One grown child has frayed sleeves, black socks (but clean feet), holes in his sweater (but intact body, though he doesn't think so). He dropped his razor in the tub so he's growing a beard; when he can afford a new razor he'll shave it off. I tell him he can love his father and still not trust him. After I say this he says his chest hurts and he has to leave the table. Dinner is soft and bland because I have a stomach bug. He eats soft and bland with appetite, as much as he wants there is. He takes seconds and thirds and what he can't eat takes home. I'm doing crosswords to move my life off the dime. If I wrote this in lines would it be more, or less, musical.

My Sister-in-law Leatrice

I wonder if Mother suspects I read the book I sent her for her birthday before I sent it. She read in the red leather chair in the foyer, Daddy in the room with the piano. My brother and I looked alike. A woman on the subway we took to music school asked if we were twins. He played well and I didn't. So why would I sit at the piano with so much longing, as if to stake a claim. Across from the middle school field—expecting to get away with it, willing to run if I have to. And I have to. We have to. It's not really stealing. It's not that I don't pity her loneliness, her reading so many novels with such poor vision. If I had her veritable blindness I'd apply for disability but she doesn't need the money, I do. Then she says when I ask Mother did you get the book, yes I have a lot of books, adding that Leatrice, my sister-in-law, says the author is a good writer. Leatrice the know-it-all, me the hit-and-miss purchaser. Carpe diem. The piano I own once had the light wood of the piano how could I steal. The stained keys of the piano played by the languorous passionate woman in of course the foreign movie assured me ivory yellows even with proper care. Yes sex outside marriage was okay in the early 1900's and between men and men and women and women. She was the one with black cleaning ladies. Oh she was nice to them: hand-me-downs my rich cousins had handed down to me, food for their lunch on top of the refrigerator so I couldn't reach it. I don't want to be seen as a domestic, whether or not I am, particularly by the poet there at critical junctures.

A Strauss Heroine

Painters on high ladders at the townhouses across the way are calling to each other: one asks about the price of an item another is selling or has sold (or buying or has bought). I don't want to listen. What I want to do is open my door and shriek like a Strauss heroine SHUT UP. I make an appointment for fingers and, for the first time, toes with Sallie, who does my fingers and who recommended Suzette, my colorist. While doing my fingers—apparently fingers always precede toes—she says she uses Cookie, not Suzette. Not that her recommendations are sacred but I already have an appointment with Liz, her hairdresser, again at her recommendation, a switch from Jason, recommended by a woman my friend swims with, whose hair my friend, a colonial historian, says is perfect. Actually I'd decided to quit Jason before Sallie promoted Liz, having observed other hairdressers cut, each snip life or death. For that matter, if it wasn't the painter, there'd be some other interference. I'm also quitting Jason, not for persistently keeping me waiting but for what he went on and on about while he haphazardly clipped, moussed (having to be reminded) and blow-dried: his being a good Samaritan and donating his sperm for the impregnation of his wife Dawn-Marie's childless sister. He mentioned a turkey baster and said, with his slight twang, he draws the line at anything more personal. That was the last straw, his drawing that line. Clients at the nail salon sit on benches that make me think of sitting shiva. At my father's shiva we sat on my brother's leather furniture and I talked about the past with my cousins—the cousin who cried at his bar mitzvah used the unfamiliar word arbitrage. These painters paint and paint and talk and talk. When they've moved on to their next job, what will distract me, what outside interference that becomes as much the main narrative as the main narrative. What is the main narrative.

Suicided Novelist

She was depressed about people dying of AIDS, the young writer whose death, probably suicide, this writer reads in an obituary. I'd thought her successful: published novelist, teacher at good schools. Imagined her pretty. Last night I stared at two women in the Indian restaurant we were trying for the first time. One woman joined her date after he'd been waiting for 15 or 20 minutes. He'd already ordered; when she arrived their food was served. I overheard her explaining she'd been on the phone with her ex-boyfriend, arguing. I found her beautiful. Delicate, thin, refined. Soft. As far from me as two people can be, except we're both women. The other woman I saw through a space between the artificial plants separating our part of the restaurant and hers. She wore a blue smock-like dress, what I could see of it, and had a nose I decided could have been Jewish. She was with an Asian man I didn't think she was married to. Her arms were heavy, her neck and chin firm. Her full breasts could have been the dress. Maybe she was pregnant. I would like the people I care about to care about me with the passion of grief. This week my son, with us at the restaurant, will have a barium test for his esophagus. He is more obsessed with disease than I and each time I see him he's heavier. By mistake he left his doggie bag at the restaurant: some of my Tandoori chicken and two pieces of that wonderful Indian bread nan.

Lucia di Lammermoor

Karen Horney, too, had a brother her parents favored. And indeed she argued with Freud about penis envy—his male opportunities, not his penis, women envy. I'm waiting for Howard, whose shoes are caked with plaster, to finish the trim on the alcove outside my study and build the shelf in the upstairs closet. Then the lady painter with the extraordinary green eyes can paint and Howard could put the doorknob without a lock back on my study door. The man I live with comments that Lucia's brother may be the reason I call *Lucia di Lammermoor* my favorite opera. I thought her mad aria the reason. I don't tell my mother to go to hell. I phone her as she expects, although she criticizes me, although she ignores me. Until my son got a reputation, winning literary awards, getting published in the *New Yorker*, he was ignored by my brother. I'm of course ignored but I take my brother and sister-in-law to lunch when they're in San Francisco. I'm still looking for an anorak as nice as the khaki Burberry my sister-in-law wore the last chilly lunchtime. I'd just had dental work and I ate the excellent food slowly. After lunch, in their quaint room with a window seat, my brother interrogated me at length about my youngest son, whose disorders interest him. Having a son with disorders judged implacable, I felt doomed. The construction workers, whose flagrantly demotic speech can't be overheard at this minute, are out front at their truck doing something noisy with all that stuff they dump in: cut-up floor and wallboards, wood siding, nails, pipes, plaster and so on. My mother said yesterday that the construction dust could enter my lungs and I immediately began worrying about pneumonia, the disease my father kept on getting and nearly dying from. His mother died of TB, yet he smoked pipes and cigars, exposing us, incidentally, to secondhand smoke. Lucia's brother lies to her bridegroom that her madness is grief at the death of her mother. My mother has made me an outcast among mother lovers.

Ulysses

When we embraced this time, I felt that embrace, one particular embrace, after running to meet each other from opposite ends of a Brooklyn subway platform, having been apart two or three months. Whether or not he is the same boy he was 40 years ago, to me he is. After drinking Calistogas in the museum cafeteria to moisten our dry mouths, we walked to the Russian restaurant he knew about and ordered the same lunch: rather I ordered what he'd ordered, but the meats—salmon, trout, whitefish—were too salty (I am not the girl I was) so after eating some I offered him the rest. We both drank iced Russian tea. The waiter told me Russian tea is black tea with whole currants for sweetness. We held each other before we left the restaurant and walked hand in hand like sweethearts on the walk back to the museum, where he picked up his car for the drive to Boston for his *Ulysses* seminar (did I really introduce him to Joyce). He looked at me in the restaurant mirror, "to remember you from all angles," he said. "It would have been a tough marriage, for you, tough for *you*," he explained. Has anyone but this man ever imagined my life. On the phone the next day I questioned him about grief—did he feel any, not 40 years ago, I know about his grief 40 years ago, yesterday's. Yes of course he felt grief, and he revised his opinion of the success of the marriage that never took place: it would have had a chance. To assuage my pain I asked him about his and I did feel better. His wife doesn't know we met or that we write and talk on the phone. She knows he wrote to me and I answered but not that there are letters now and exchanged poems now and regular phone calls now. I was hurt by a husband's infidelity. I am flirting with what I condemned him for.

Princess Elizabeth

In exchange for safety, remembering that the survivor of a plane crash said he prayed, I promised I'd fast. Yes I would fast. My bargain, which I half believed I'd keep, telling myself this time I would keep it, seemed reasonable, not as excessive as offering to be good forever. Failing, again, to keep my word, I would like to come up with a sacrifice that would convey my integrity to whom (what) I halfheartedly and in calm as well as threatening moments acknowledge as that force responsible for the unexplainable, not only origin. I am a silly, frightened woman, have lived long enough (if helplessly) to recognize patterns beyond pain and pleasure, the grinding pains, the milling pleasures, of day after day. I'm at Z. Already, minutes later, I've forgotten today's Z. Is there no one in this classy town who is dirty or without a limb or grotesquely obese. Could I for just a while stop doing what I am afraid ever to stop doing, I mean writing. In the middle of the lake I chickened out and turned back, letting the fear hypotenuse take over the rash, brave straight line. Never again going in water over my head. So many clean people without visible defects. Such good manners—gray hair man in blue tee picking up spaghetti with fork and spoon, opening mouth to receive perfect amount, not too much or too little, not one strand escaping expertly twirled ball. I could give to a charity—I'm serious—could teach without pay at a safe jail or a home for wayward adolescents. Automatically, bargaining, you see yourself as possessing something extra. Someone is lower than you. How many unfortunates there are, how many worse-offs. A mother singles out the exquisite child whose hard death she'll bring about, partly starvation. There you are, going to the party in your Princess Elizabeth dress, a bow in your curls.

Morty's Ex-Wife

Mother would like to give me her expensive shoes but we wear different sizes so she doesn't press. I wonder if I would have taken them once. Shopping, we'd go the whole day and end up with shoelaces and hair ribbons. We were looking for shoes to go with my new chartreuse suit and could find only brown suede platforms with very high heels and ankle straps. I wore the suit and platforms (with ankle straps) to my cousin's wedding, towering over everyone. I was the tallest person at her wedding, a single sunflower on a sculptured lawn in my chartreuse suit and platforms with ankle straps. I danced with my father and brother, looking down on my father's bald spot and my tall brother's thin brown hair. Arlyne said I should wear shoes with heels and ankle straps (she wore wedgies). She told me I had good legs and should show them off. I have been trying to find Arlyne. I found her ex-husband's obituary but she wasn't mentioned and she isn't in the New York phone books, either her maiden or married name. She and Morty were angry at me for not going to their wedding. The day I visited the Queens apartment dominated by the piano Morty played while Arlyne and I tried to settle our differences, he barely talked to me. I wanted a jacket for the cold. The weekend before the wedding, when it was already cold, I went home so my parents could buy me one. They persuaded me to write Arlyne and sent me back to college with a lightweight red jacket that didn't keep out the unforgiving cold.

Proust

I don't know what friends know, for instance, what postmodernism really is, and deconstruction. Many words in Proust I have to look up; some I write in a notebook I began 2/3 into volume one. I have my own ideas—if I lectured to a group of academics still with long hair in the nineties I'd be attacked. Did my grandmother notice me. Proust's young narrator knocks on the wall between his room and his grandmother's to tell her he is ready for his milk. He taps lightly three times and she taps three times to say she's heard and is coming. To be liked by my aunt and uncle, I acted cheerful and younger than my age, almost like a slave who doesn't want to be sold away from her children. I stayed with them when my parents went to the city. I wandered around the unkempt garden, ate my aunt's heavy food, read my cousin's few books. A book with a yellow cover I read over and over— an orphan sent to live with her relatives becomes their servant: cleaning, weeding, milking.

Shirley

The voice downstairs that assuredly didn't speak its first words in English is from a bank card center and for some reason, by some fluke, I have charged again though I thought I hadn't and know I shouldn't. Upstairs I hear the voice scold something like you shouldn't have but you did, just don't do it again. Though I am late for aerobics, I play the voice while I rinse my teacup and put teacup and saucer in the dishwasher. I was right, the voice has a pronounced accent, and wrong, it is not from a bank card center, it is from the car rental place and the reason my car didn't have air conditioning (which the voice, a young woman, calls "air") is that I rented the cheapest car and the cheapest car doesn't come with air. It will be a scorcher. I tell Ruth, who asks if anything is wrong when I keep leaving class so I won't have a heart attack, the hot weather gets to me. It also gets to Norma, who needs surgery for her ulcer. We don't know each other's last names. Ruth's is McDermott. I know because it's on the envelope she hands me on my way back from the drinking fountain. The envelope contains information about an eye device like a TV screen her husband, Charles McDermott, reads with. I'd like my mother to know about this eye device. My mother's bad eyes have left my bad eyes behind. She used to say she was cockeyed, meaning she had bad eyes, when I was the one with bad eyes and cockeyed, meaning cross-eyed. Shirley's husband and two kids threw Shirley, dead a month, a party because she'd have liked that. The table with her lace tablecloth had enough food for her wedding. I wanted to leave but my husband said since we came we should talk to Shirley's husband, outside, wearing a white dress shirt and a tie. I'd rather have seen Shirley's husband wearing shorts on that scorcher, smoking a cigarette outside on that scorcher in his usual shorts.

Grace Kelly

Selling cheesecake can be a vehicle. (I refuse to call them veggies.) Sour cream cheesecake with ricotta (pot cheese). Selling services. Selling services which I buy—his wonderful clothes make me trust him to help me. Even exchange—the seller receives as much. The St. Michael's Alley cheesecake I understand should be the dessert of choice. But I chose the strawberry-raspberry tart. (I'd like cheesecake now.) "Do not forsake me, oh my darling, on this our wedding day." Gary Cooper leaves Grace Kelly and I am certain he will be killed. The first time I see the movie, the summer of my wedding, I am certain. The second time I hope, since I know he won't be killed, that I won't expect it to happen, that I won't look ahead with foreboding suspiciously like depression, that I won't be surprised, even grateful, when it doesn't happen. I kept expecting it to happen, kept looking ahead with foreboding suspiciously like depression, and when it didn't happen was surprised, even grateful. I'd bought the fiction. Haven't bought what poet offers—must renounce him, buy elsewhere.

Doris Lessing

Afraid of tripping, I concentrate on fallen cones and branches, on puddles, and look sideways at the houses I imagine people with money live in—I can't imagine living in one. On a side street the modern cement color house I've noticed before and like, the unpleasing angles out of character here, I can't imagine living in either, and I am reminded of the architecturally advanced mishmash rooms of the Cambridge house I stayed in one summer with a boyfriend unenamoured with me. On the main street leading from freeway to town, I look not as much at the mansions on one side, remodeled unsuccessfully or left in their former, depressing, splendour, not at all at cars on the other side, fewer than usual since it is raining, enough for an umbrella—I've never chosen to walk in the rain before. In town, shops and no houses, I have my reward, a raisin scone and a cappuccino, the steamed milk, which I sprinkle with too much chocolate, not enough cinnamon, unfortunately mixing with the coffee, diluting it. Doris Lessing left her two children when she went off to do her thing, which included writing. The girl with freckles and short dark hair, who said she saw us at Kepler's the night last spring my son read from his book, brings me my fruit plate: cantaloupe, honeydew, pineapple, strawberries—I eat only the cantaloupe, maybe a bite of honeydew and a bite of pineapple, no unripe strawberries. This man I've known almost 20 years, who I sometimes think knows more about me than I know, is who I keep seeing all over town. He doesn't look like himself. He's wearing a turtleneck, not his usual jacket and tie, and he's wider around the middle than he is, like a different son, who doesn't exercise but plans to. No he isn't himself and like most of the people you never really see, only think you see, with a face I don't recognize, without associations, as impossible as that may seem.

Cassandra and Irene

I vowed I would not have ugly, pendulous breasts like my mother's under her ripped nightgowns and housecoats but I do. Here's one reason for her anger: I didn't leave the writing colony to take care of her when she came home from the hospital. She didn't want anyone else, only me, and I didn't come to Florida, I stayed at the writing colony and worried I had skin cancer and dreamed about animals biting me and shared the bathroom with a Nobel chemist who ate cheese and bread for breakfast because that's what he ate as a child in Europe. He was a Jew Hitler hadn't gotten and I had diarrhea every day in the shared bathroom, mortified at the smell. When I was a girl in love with Mrs. Vanderpool, my strict teacher, my best friend Elise Gruber and I walked up and down the street across from Mrs. Vanderpool's private house with a glassed-in front porch, 10 blocks from Elise's apartment building and mine, each with 6 floors. Once, walking without Elise, I saw Mrs. Vanderpool leave her house and thought she saw me. Cassandra in the poem in my father's Louis Untermeyer told the truth and was ignored—wasn't I like her with my two dresses and my settling accounts in my head at night before my brother came to his twin bed. In Ellenville in the forties the summer I was knitting a vest with two colors, light blue and brown, that I would never finish, though I knit every day with pregnant spectacled Rita Fox—I also wore spectacles—whose husband was in the Pacific—it was the summer before the end of the war or it was the summer the war ended—I saw *King's Row* with Ronald Reagan and a beautiful girl who will lose her mind and whose name is Cassandra. I surely wept in that movie. There is a poet whose name is Irene and my maiden name but we are not related. My allergist's name is also Irene and an editor in Ithaca, nowhere near Ellenville, is Irene also. I am obsessed with Irene, the name of the poet, perhaps a distant relative, of the allergist, of the Ithaca editor—I mean when I see or hear Irene I get a frisson of recognition. These days I only cry when I am humiliated or defeated, at the end of my rope. I am drawn to Cassandra and Irene for the sound, possibly only for the sound—Cassie—even the sobriquet has a good sound—and I sometimes believe when I hear Cassandra or Irene, Irene more than Cassandra, that the name is mine, that's what the frisson is about, oh I'm not really sure. A soft afternoon early in my marriage to a Jew exiled by Hitler like the laureate, we happened to see a silly Doris Day movie in a working-class neighborhood adjacent to ours near the university press where I was a clerk-typist hoping to advance to editor—but I didn't advance, I was fired—and that unlikely afternoon—we didn't usually go to afternoon movies—I glimpsed a contentment I hadn't even considered, let alone had access to, how the body could give pleasure without the intercession of, say, something like the mind or even desire, a sweetness like Doris Day and kitschy melodies that I could walk to the way I walked down the movie aisle when I was three or so to the actress who'd said "Come here little girl" and I thought she meant me. It hurt to have sex and I kept putting it off and when we got home that barely dark spring evening to our tiny apartment with the cracked linoleum and the bathroom we shared with romping newlyweds from Australia I was in one of my gray, formless Sunday moods so I cooked Sunday dinner, which concluded with chocolate chip cookies I'd made the day before, mixing the batter in the miraculous new Sunbeam Mixmaster, then we turned on the radio for one of our Sunday programs and did or didn't have sex, it doesn't matter.

Mussolini and Others

———

———

———

———

———

Mussolini, Mary Karr, Michael Ryan, Margaret Johnson, Ben Aldrich, Heather McHugh, Hitler

We are sitting at the kitchen table playing dominoes. My father is talking about Mussolini. I don't know how to play dominoes but I am playing dominoes and I know my father is angry and worried about war in distant Ethiopia. Dominoes is the game Mary Karr's father and buddies play in the *The Liars' Club*, the book I've barely begun. I like finishing books I've begun or else I'd start *Everybody's Autobiography*. Maybe I should have bought Michael Ryan's red memoir. Margaret Johnson's pretty hair is pale yellow. We eat mediocre Chinese food we agree is good in a Cambridge, Massachusetts restaurant. They pay $3 for a babysitter. To eat mediocre Chinese food we agree is good will cost Margaret Johnson and Ben Aldrich $12, which they can't afford. Margaret sings in a church choir. Her work is less conventional than mine. I would like my work to be less conventional. My father doesn't call Mussolini tyrant, dictator, bully. He teases me into a goodnight kiss when, for the first time, years before dominoes and Mussolini, I assert this night I will not kiss him goodnight. I kiss him, quenching my igneous essence. The book I got igneous from, Heather McHugh recommended at a reading. For almost a year, when my father's bearded father dies, we do not listen to the radio. I was expecting not to have the radio turned on for a year but towards the end of the year my father turned it on, probably for war news, a later war, Mussolini now a buddy of Hitler, a dictator my father mentions as a dictator but not as a dictator particularly malevolent towards Jews, who we are. My father, my brother, I, who don't know how to play dominoes, play dominoes. That I don't know how makes me uneasy, uneasiness I accept. My mother is fiddling with food and pots in a room a movie could reproduce beautifully, yellow indoor light exposing at the oilcloth-covered kitchen table my father, my brother, me, then from my father, looking down at his dominoes, Mussolini.

25

André Gide

In the Resistance, the woman says, they were given the name of someone already safe should they be interrogated. For a while she successfully eluded Nazi nets. I have observed that people who have suffered a great deal are readily moved to tears. Years after the Nazis, the unlined face of another woman in the Resistance—evil can't adhere to it like a postage stamp with insufficient glue. Patricia Hamm, whose name suddenly comes to me, endured many skin peelings for acne without marked results, maybe because she continued eating potato chips and then penitently sleeping through meals for one to two days (I see Patricia Hamm from the Midwest as if we still lived in the dormitory, our rooms facing). The woman who had been married to a very rich man lived, I remember, in an exclusive wooded area not far from the tract house where my life was falling apart. After we spent an afternoon exchanging our similar and different histories she moved and wanting to speak to her I called both her office and new house a number of times, leaving messages, but she never called back. In the Bronx, for instance, the boy on a high floor pressed the button for the elevator and when the door without the elevator opened he fell to his death. Likewise, continues the man on the radio, a woman with AIDS goes to a Bronx hospital emergency room. She waits and waits but the first night no bed is available and the second night, after she'd sat up the entire first night, she is given a stretcher in the corridor to sleep on but it is covered with bloody sheets. By comparison, my friend, a Catholic, is reading the journals of André Gide, who didn't write compulsively, he played the piano compulsively. I've told my friend about my playing the piano. I wish I had more time to play the piano but I also write and I wish I had more time to write but I also play the piano. Bewildered, hearing unvarying pigeon shrieks, I got up from the piano. I saw that the pigeon (it had so much blue in its feathers) was on the deck, stuck like a blob of chewing gum. The pigeons have been excreting like crazy there, especially in one corner. The pigeon was motionless but not dead. To remove it, I trapped it in a carton I threw off the deck; when the carton landed the pigeon walked away. The next day the handyman, who commiserates with me about the pigeon shit I scrub like Sisyphus, says he found a dead pigeon near the mailboxes.

Samuel Beckett

That day a young boy about 8 or 9 was sitting in a green zippered see-through child carrier on the back of a bike. Was there something wrong with him, too big and old for this carrier with a bright red bow. Was he playing with what was not his, his mother unable to control him, his mother not Samuel Beckett's mother to leave and come back to, leave and come back to. And under an umbrella a man was feeding a little boy in a wheelchair and laughing, almost cooing. At first I didn't see the wheelchair, just the laughing face of the man and the blank pale face of the boy, his hair a middle-aged man's, the wheelchair like the unforeshadowed next scene of a movie, I see a lot of movies. Troubled and anxious, I went on walking to the pen store, troubled and anxious that day apart from both boys, the bike boy and the wheelchair boy, as I had been before them both, bike boy and wheelchair boy, went on walking in the late afternoon of that intensely spring day knowing I was walking and that the day was like every day except it felt exceptional. At the pen store I bought ink cartridges and pencil erasers, tried an automatic pencil I didn't buy and looked at a pen holder I didn't buy for the pen I already have and a pen holder I didn't buy for that pen and its matching automatic pencil, which I hadn't tried. The foreign-name salesperson so willing to help with small purchases and items you don't purchase spoke with the accent of her country, whatever it was, and I thought of Lotte, my sister-in-law's painter sister, her accent from a different country, or was it a lisp, a slight lisp Lotte also has. Lotte is brave because she paints without certainty and I am brave too. In the window of a ritzy department store a mannequin in a long filmy green dress with a scarf prompts a woman to say green to the man she is walking with, probably her husband, green to the man with a boy, probably their son, no impairments visible.

Harriet Feigenbaum Is a Sculptor

She is building a model of a concentration camp complex. She has not been to a camp but has seen an aerial model. What she noticed: the symmetry, the exactness. As maids place pillows (these are Harriet Feigenbaum's ideas, images), so was the concentration camp complex: orderly, but not in relation to a plan. The commandant's house with its kitchen was in the center—surrounded, then, by the ovens, gas chambers. In high school, several of my teachers' wives were in mental hospitals (asylums). No one said why, but it was understood they had started menopause and gone mad. One felt pity for these men, still devoted to their crazy, absent wives. I am post-menopausal. My doctor, Chinese, finds it difficult to examine my heavy breasts for lumps. The ob-gyn I went to for an abortion when I was pregnant, at 40, vigorously palpated my breasts for milk, maybe (to give him the benefit of the doubt) to see how far along I was. He hurt me. My Uncle Nat Lemler was a prison guard. My Aunt Jeannie was the least attractive of all my mother's sisters. Not that they were beauties, but she had absolutely no beauty, almost as if she deserved the terrible man she was married to, who would divorce her, the first divorce in the family. I felt terrible seeing Aunt Jeannie, who lived in poverty, as the ugly duckling of my mother's large family. The Vietnam War Memorial was created by an artist who was not a veteran. Reconnecting with a man I loved 40 years ago, the chance for a new start and new loss. Terrible dreams too disgusting to write.

Harry Levin's Shakespeare

Todd was going to a dance and was nervous because he needed to meet somebody. When he has diarrhea, he calls his mother and she picks him up. She doesn't pick him up after an epileptic fit. Weren't you nervous at dances, I ask my new husband, who moonlights at Pizza Hut for Todd's agency. You have to relax, he told Todd, you're more likely to meet somebody, relaxed. Richard, who would become a District Attorney, told Emilie he'd like to meet me. We were all taking Harry Levin's Shakespeare. The day she introduced us I had on a red corduroy vest and knee socks. I should have fallen in love with Richard but he was too tall. But when I danced with him, tall as he was, I danced like a sophomore who liked to dance, who took social dancing only to satisfy the P.E. requirement, not to learn to dance. Emilie and I were talking on the second floor of a house in Brookline about her breakdown the year before. She had a wry sense of humor and knew Richard from the year before the year before. I had been in love with a different Richard and had come close to a breakdown myself. Emilie lived in the dorms. Ann lived in Dorchester. Her father, a podiatrist, quarreled with her mother in the car, the four of us going to the zoo on a chilly, gloomy Sunday afternoon. Ann was a Chemistry major; so was Emilie a Chemistry major; probably so was Richard, the future District Attorney. After his prom, on the floor of some dark living room in Newton or Mattapan, the gowned and tuxed couples necked and petted. Not Richard and I. The kid who installs my bookshelves takes out his contacts in my wallpapered bathroom, the wallpaper pretty but not hung right. The walls should have been muddied and I should have had them stripped and muddied and the wallpaper rehung when there was money.

Alexander Pope

In a crowded hall I would not expect the lecturer to notice me but she does. She has her assistant bring in electrical equipment to help me record the program and hear it better, which is what I could have used listening to the mezzo in the car outside the café. A pregnant woman quite far along, without a helmet, actually rode off on a bike. Up and down streets people stroll, in no hurry to get anywhere, hospitals or homes, including their own, or entertainments, including operas. Anyway I easily get the equipment to work—this also surprises me but not the lecturer, who suspiciously resembles a minor poet who consistently has ignored me, although she did send me to a famous male poet, who helped me in the beginning, I suppose, and I don't have to use so many commas. I do not understand the crimes I have committed or that I even consider them crimes since they are only crimes because they have led to criminal consequences. Outside the lecture hall a woman I would want to be or am, as the word marriage implies, has someone else's tweezed eyebrows and I can imagine her in my daughter's white beret. Talk about crimes—I let myself be put down and let myself be put down. Age is not a crime although it feels like it as I stroll like a ghost up and down thronged streets. I understand the alter ego in her meticulously governed daily life is religious to the point of orthodoxy, like my daughter's insistence on her diet—imagine nothing but fruit until noon, no sweets after 4, no protein and starch combined, ice cream chanced only on an empty stomach. The belief is that interrupting digestion complicates intake: everything depends on digestion, trickier than supposed, as I know. Now you'd think a baby should have no problems in that area but although I would take adequate care of one that precious I will leave if I have to. Periods cannot be eliminated as easily. Let's say the lecture is on Alexander Pope, which it wouldn't be. Maybe Donne—

what about a woman. Or, for me, dashes. Not even the discount department store, where I hoped to buy cheap undies, is open for business. The amazing thing is the lecturer I could have been if male or content to be minor isn't put off by my ostensible crimes: what were they—leading passersby down blind alleys where they could be attacked, consequences again, a function of colons. It's not that I had no appetite as a child but that I was hungry at the wrong times and for the wrong foods (parentheses are almost always avoidable).

Walt Whitman

My mother accompanied me to the ceremony where I got my prize money (I think $5) and certificate, surname misspelled and unpronounceable. I think I won second but it could have been third. I wanted to win but I hadn't asked God because I no longer prayed, even to keep my family and relatives and relatives of relatives alive. I had dreaded bedtime, the necessity of those prayers. In bed, before going to sleep, I memorized the essay. As the room darkened (it was late spring and I went to bed while it was light) I selected images and words: we had had the title, "How to Win the War Effort," for weeks. I thought to make my point without making my point, using the words and pictures I knew were right. I chose for the pleasure of the right words and pictures. I wrote prose as if it were poetry, having in mind *Leaves of Grass* by Walt Whitman, a poet I wanted to write like. My mother and I took several subway trains to what I think of as a courtroom in downtown Brooklyn but it might have been Manhattan. I believe a judge awarded the prizes and I remember a long walk from my seat in the back to his bench. Maybe we sat in the back because we came in late. We could have come in late. Or the judge could have been a woman and a woman clerk could have called my name, not mispronounced, read correctly from the shameful misspelling on the certificate. I don't remember words my mother and I exchanged in the courtroom or on the trains from section to section of the city: perhaps we didn't speak. I conceived the essay, wrote it in my head and said it by heart before my brother came to bed in the room we shared, by then thoroughly dark. I wrote and memorized for weeks. I hoped I would win a prize; it weakened as it went on, I didn't hope for first prize. I cared only about the opening battlefield paragraphs, to make them perfect.

Girl Boys Shoved Broomstick Up

Basically your body is between you and everyone, especially the doctor. Sometimes I think it is thin and shapely. Sometimes I am sitting and I realize I must concentrate if I want to sit straight. Twice last week I fell, slipping on a leaf on a wet walkway. I should ride the exercise bike every day. To stay awake in movies I drink coffee and coke and can't fall asleep at two in the morning. Before going to bed I read the accounts of women raped by Serbian soldiers. Daughters in front of mothers and fathers. Raped and some killed. Virgins. Old women. I read again about the retarded girl who hoped for a date so she let high school boys shove a bat and then a broomstick up her after first shoving her own five fingers up. They lined up chairs like the movies, the same boys who'd made her eat dog feces when she was younger. My body embarrasses my gynecologist—I can tell. I have insurance but to see a doctor when I'm sick I have to assert myself. Yesterday at Blue Sky the potatoes were cold and tasteless and the muffin inedible. The waitress with skinny legs who wears shorts all year round said one of the cooks was in jail. On the way to our car after the opera we pass a woman sitting under quilts in the rain.

Dr. J

I told my mother I'm thinking of using our family name. I thought she'd be pleased. She wanted to know why I don't take my husband's name, meaning my new husband. Women aren't doing that, I said. It *is* my name, I said. Dr. J, the university psychiatrist, addressed me as Miss followed by that name she pronounced like German each time she beckoned me to her office from the hallway where I'd been waiting impatiently for her to finish with Helen Margolis, Jill Stocker, Hanna Kirchheimer or Janet (whose last name I've forgotten). Dr. J's office looked out on a Harvard Square side street. Once I saw someone I knew out the window and she came from behind her large desk and looked out the window with me. It might have been the German boyfriend with a famous name she thought I should break up with. She also thought I shouldn't marry the man whose difficult German name I gladly took. Now we're not married and he has given that name and an ostentatious diamond in an antique, kitschy setting to a big-breasted woman with a cute first name. It is almost as big as my mother's, but his big-breasted blond's clothes don't go with that diamond: loose trench coat and flat, soiled nurse's shoes.

Bette Davis

I sort of remembered the scene with blond Anne Baxter in a satin nightgown, unwrinkled though Anne had been in bed. Montgomery Clift smelled fresh without cologne, you could tell. Anne and Montgomery, their eyes reflecting longing like tin in the sun, held each other as I've only held and been held once—well, maybe more than once. Is this soft passion, not seen in movies anymore, maybe, therefore, not felt. The year before *I Confess* I stayed at the Chateau Frontenac for 2 honeymoon nights. Light in cities, because broken, in the movie by severely slanted streets, is beautiful. Country light is plainer and seems distilled—what do I mean—I don't mean distilled, I mean thinner because spread out, uninterrupted. If I never saw another movie I wouldn't perish. If I lived in the middle of nowhere I wouldn't perish. In 1953 I heard T. S. Eliot read, one of the first fans pressing into Sanders Theatre. It snowed the Saturday of Doris Keeble's baby shower. She had 3 maternity outfits, 2 for work, 1 for dress. I remember Frontenac's expensive bed. Did I visit Quebec as a child. Or only Montreal. I could ask my mother. How tough life is— and not for the reasons we think—for the reluctant acceptance of flaws, in ourselves too. I remember less and less, like the light all of a sudden fading for Bette Davis in *Dark Victory*. Since *Dark Victory*, when the lights have dimmed in restaurants, my house—anywhere, without fail—I have immediately checked to see that they were actually dimming, not just for me with a brain tumor. On the Canadian trip, the 2nd one, we ran out of money, and my father, who in my memory had never eaten ham and would never eat ham again, in more than one restaurant, our money almost gone (unless it was the 1st trip, although I believe it was the 2nd), ordered a ham sandwich, saying jambon, showing off jambon, with a straight face jambon, just jambon, jambon surrounded by correct English, jambon.

Disney

Father and son had red hair. Father was lean and we never spoke though he lived next door. After he died his wife told a neighbor in my presence that at his physical just a few weeks before he had been pronounced in perfect health. I thought I should visit the funeral parlor, remembering my somber but not gloomy parents going off after supper to visit mourners sitting on boxes, a difficult obligation, another of their demonstrable moral victories, though of course there was no body to view. I looked from the neighbor in his white casket to his wife, as white as her off-white dress. I felt like crying, felt how imminent crying was, though I had cared not a whit for this man alive. How frightened I am of dying. At about that time I went to the doctor with worries about my heart. What I was worried about of course wasn't my physical heart but my capacity to connect to people, to care about them, to love them. A neighbor who was gravely ill, whose heart gave out, had sought my friendship and I'd denied her. And there was more, there was sex, for instance. You'll never be the same, I said to myself in the funeral parlor. I went into the early fall evening, October, I think, the small city I never would be at home in, and I felt unable to enjoy being alive. It takes 1 year for the earth to complete its movement around the sun. The dead man's daughter (actually his wife's daughter) married a truck driver who bit their daughter when she misbehaved. In early womanhood the other daughter of the dead father with red hair, his daughter by birth, had her voluminous breasts surgically reduced and on the verge of menopause her sister, who'd abandoned the idea of college, eloping with the truck driver and going to Disneyland for the weekend instead, had a mastectomy.

Greta Garbo in Queens

I'd been kept young, a virgin, only pseudo-modern, yet my desires, he saw. Both my mother and I find confrontation excruciating. On trains at night, I'm afraid I'll be stranded. You know what it's like not to be lost by being lost. Only 4 years older but fatherly, and sexual, he'd occasionally kiss me. You can't predict who will succumb to plainness, who soar. This week, in Sunnyvale, not Brooklyn, I start a Bach Invention. I remember taking the train to Queens on a week-end when they were already married and already unhappy, she per-haps having yielded to her other, perhaps stronger, love of women. No kissing. We're estranged too. It is too late to make amends and at the piano while my friend and I talk on the couch he barely tolerates my presence, retaining anger with integrity. She looked like Greta Garbo. I looked Jewish but didn't think I looked enough anything. She could do what she wanted and her mother, to my eyes an old woman, made salami sandwiches with lettuce and mayonnaise. I'd never had a salami sandwich with lettuce and mayonnaise and found it delicious and rebelled with my friend, eating her lunch at 10 a.m. in French. Why did the soulful French teacher's husband walk out on her soon after they married. I understood for that reason her flesh had softened and spread and tears would gather at inappropriate times, say at the choice of Guillaume and Babette—my French name, I've forgotten. A composer who would be famous, he explicated what his teachers taught as if I'd understand: he saw me as a writer, desire stripped of delay. Try this: put perception that you've wasted your life in an impossible slogan like dropping a green oversized Asian cup and it doesn't break. What I needed to be forgiven for is giving up without a fight. Religious control through ritual ties hands, pre-vents breakdown; adhering to form, though not to the tee, delays the void. My friend and I saw a movie, I think Hepburn, a rainy Sunday in Coney Island, the music Brahms, the 1st or 3rd, the opening phrase repeated backwards: da da *da/da* da da. Then too I lived somewhere else, Flatbush, not Brighton Beach, like Sunnyvale, not New York.

—in memory of Morton Feldman

Tiny Tim

Does it matter that the young woman in the row ahead had long red hair deeper than the darkest red tomato sauce, almost the color of blood. That the cherry blossoms on Stevens Creek would never be perfect again. That sweat is colorless. I remember the peach fabric of my high school graduation dress (was my mother already gray). I wore a blue wool bathing suit that summer. The incredibly obese man two rows in back with a white shirt, khaki trousers and black dress shoes made ominous noises so we moved to the row behind the young woman with red hair. The man who took our tickets had yellow hair like straw, wild like Tiny Tim's. Many were smoking in the lobby. I had asked the young woman with dyed blond hair at Double Rainbow for a taste of pralines and cream. Purposely did not ask the young man in a curly black wig. It was drizzling and since we had ice cream cones (mine, vanilla) we hurried into Walgreen's and looked for a toothbrush. I worried about my steel gray car parked outside the Gap close to the crosswalk. In the window colorful tee shirts I wouldn't mind wearing. A student having cancer surgery Christmas Eve day brought me a plant wrapped in red foil as if I were the one having surgery. As I pass the truck with junk food, red apples and orange spice tea I imagine her (we have the same name) walking into class or waiting outside with the two men who like my encouraging teaching methods. The brother-in-law of one is a poet in our royal blue anthology. That the lover of the woman once in chartreuse was murdered, after the movie doesn't matter.

The Other Phyllis

Elsa, a psychoanalyst with an accent, who drove me home the day my Honda was in the shop, was arguing. The aerobics music drowned the words but we could tell she was arguing, loud enough for Deb, the instructor, to stop doing pliés and look in her direction. Deb was wearing her leotard with large black circles that isn't especially flattering. Elsa's aerobics outfits match, even the towels she brings for floor work, even her many aerobics shoes. The girl with black tights and a black leotard, who wanted the fan on, told Elsa, who didn't want the fan on, to move. Elsa, her first class after 8 weeks out for a tennis injury, stayed where she was, explaining to the girl in black all the spaces away from the fan were taken and she didn't want the breeze on her recovered muscles so she'd be out another 8 weeks. When we were doing abs on the smelly blue mats the club insists it washes regularly, I saw a fellow with metal glasses and a big white tee shirt reach over and touch Elsa's antagonist's foot sympathetically and I began to feel sorry for Elsa, for her need for assertion, for its consequences at the club. After class the other Phyllis and a few of us who are over 50 followed Elsa to the desk. Sweat like tears still rolling down her flushed cheeks, she explained her position and we supported her like family. Deb came by the desk in a long sweatshirt covering her unfortunate leotard and Elsa repeated her story to Deb, who said she didn't blame Elsa. I personally believe Deb did blame Elsa. As a matter of fact, though I was sympathetic this time, I nurse antagonism when Elsa pushes me out of my front-center spot after she comes in late with her matching outfits, including shoes, and her stories, often sad, of Europe and her father, a famous poet there. The other Phyllis, the oldest of us, well maybe not the oldest but the nicest, told Elsa to do herself a favor and forget the unpleasant incident, but Elsa, who remembers the exact green hue of the SS guards' uniforms, I'm sorry to say the exact green hue of tights I, one of the lucky Jews, once wore to aerobics, said she would not forget it. The other Phyllis claims she isn't worried about her biopsy, that the painless shadow on her mammogram could be nothing. But I'm worried about Phyllis's biopsy. I admit it, I'm worried about the other Phyllis's biopsy.

Glenn Gould

The upstairs bedroom over the garage had been our son's, before that a playroom for all four children. It had dark wood panelling, real wood. An orange plaid couch opened to a bed. The mother's helper slept on it when my husband went to Spain, we'd bought it for the mother's helper, a college girl, to sleep on when he went to Spain. I locked the heavy accordion door to listen to Glenn Gould. What kept a couple together, our very heavy therapist had said, was sleeping together in the same bed every night. No matter what happens during the day, no matter what arguments or conflicts, you still sleep together in the same bed every night. Kitty, our next therapist, who had taken a class from my husband, assigned me a tape for homework. She believed I was afraid of penises, a phobia responsible for the sexual difficulties my husband complained about, so after I listened to Glenn Gould I turned on Kitty, whose soft flat voice assured me that I controlled the penis, that the penis would come no closer than I wanted it to. Kitty wore alluring clothes; one light color silky dress had a slit down the front. I tried to avoid Kitty's dress with a slit and to assume a compassionate face while my husband, fighting tears, told the story he had told the heavy therapist before Kitty and would tell the not-quite-as-heavy therapist after Kitty about leaving Germany just in time. One Valentine's Day we had a terrible fight—it may have been when I pulled off the window shade and threw my small round unbreakable plastic mirror on the linoleum and he called me crazy. I think Kitty made a house call, I see her sitting in the living room on the fairly new brown couch (we also had new brown wall-to-wall carpet and new brown dishes and new flatware with brown wood handles). It wasn't Valentine's, on Valentine's she had a late dinner date, I remember her mentioning her late Valentine's dinner date. Her office had gorgeous posters and prints, which reminded me she'd been married to an artist. Because of art I'm thinking of my friend, once my creative writing student, who now paints. Without her small twin boys and their slightly older brother, whom their father moved to a city she has to take a train or bus to and doesn't often, she goes down to the bottom often, but now, painting, she has a future.

Black Narcissus

Who had the birthmark, the Chinese man or the sweet innocent foolish girl he was marrying. I married a German Jew who'd seen Hitler. For my wedding I wore traditional white, including veil, changing to a blue suit and a hat like a movie bride, as bony as Katharine Hepburn. In the x-ray waiting room a woman lay dead or unconscious on a stretcher. Another woman, her scalp with stubble, sat in a wheelchair. Come to think of it, the one thing my parents didn't restrict was writing. One Sunday the movie I went to was a long way from home. It was dusk when I came out, the streets deserted. My parents were in the kitchen eating supper, it was suppertime. I sat down and ate. I couldn't believe I would do that in a movie, *Black Narcissus* with Deborah Kerr. But on the subway it is different. The man walks to the next swaying car. Nothing happens. Following my Friday afternoon piano lesson on the Lower East Side, I stopped at the delicatessen. At home my parents were eating supper, it was suppertime. I sat down and ate though I had eaten. They talked about going to the movies. I wanted them to go—I wanted my mother's happiness. A cellist, a blind date, took me to the movies, *Black Narcissus* with Deborah Kerr, and I didn't restrict his hands. With the boyfriend I loved but didn't marry I saw the movie version of *Strait is the Gate*—the music that kept repeating, as movie music does, Franck's Symphony in D. I remember sitting in the front row though we wouldn't have sat in the front row but why couldn't we have. Despite what my father believed, it was not *Black Narcissus* with Deborah Kerr, it was *Symphonie Pastorale* and my boyfriend put his arm around my shoulders or we held hands, that's all.

Anne or Ann

We've been talking on the phone for almost three years—with less intensity recently, mostly recounting anecdotes from our present, separate lives, having accepted a relationship that can't go anywhere. It wasn't the conversation in which he traced what he considered his mean streak to his dish-breaking father, to which I answered that I hadn't seen anything mean in him 40 years ago. It was the conversation two or three weeks later, two or three weeks in which I didn't call him and he didn't call me, each waiting for the attention of the other. But when I hear his voice I drop my irritation with the restraints he imposes and become a different woman, a willing girl. So when he hesitated, saying this incident from the past, from that one year we had, might upset me, I answered how could it. Home from college a weekend or vacation, I'd introduced him to a friend with a Boston accent (he thinks someone from college, I think maybe Anne, my small blond music major roommate, or the other Ann, a flirt) and he found himself seeing her as interesting, which surprised him because of the love which blinded him to anyone, anything, but me. He said, "You were jealous." He wants me to see him as mean— it was mean, he said, to tell you I found her interesting; when you said isn't she nice, I said yes, she really seems interesting—not out of innocence but meanness. And hearing him I'm surprised that having set aside the possibility of a physical relationship—at first with regret—I'm hurt, although the incident he repeated happened 40 years ago and is one of the deluge of incidents from the past I don't remember at all. Anyway, the day he showed up with his emaciated wife in her lawn party hat, I'd just learned I was pregnant.

Tall Deanna Durbin

The family that bought the partially built house next to our summer place in Kerhonkson came from the South. My father called them poor white trash. The boy and girl went barefoot. On our way home to Brooklyn from a spring or fall weekend in Kerhonkson, we dropped the father at the Brooklyn Navy Yard for his war job. During the war my father would pick up hitchhiking servicemen in our blue Plymouth, our first car, bought at Artwin Motors on Ocean Avenue from a salesman, like a detective, never without a hat. My father used Sunoco gas; there was a Sunoco station on Ocean and Avenue O. Sometimes he sang "Old Black Joe," "Swanee River," "Flow Gently Sweet Afton," "Believe Me if All Those Endearing Young Charms." I sang with him. In the prison movie I worry that the lines about the pencil box I got for my 10th birthday were accidentally dropped from my published poem. But they weren't: I cut them deliberately. Its 2 drawers contained an eraser, a ruler, small colored pencils sharpened to a point, a useless protractor, a compass, a pencil sharpener that didn't sharpen. The man spent more than 3 years in solitary and couldn't stand straight. His cheeks caved in like someone in a Walker Evans photo. The Southern girl and I played once or twice. She was younger; we had little in common. When I don't have dolls anymore, even tall Deanna Durbin I kept in her box on the shelf, I ask for a doll carriage from the Brooklyn Sears to take to Kerhonkson for the summer. One summer I imagined hitting the ball on a rubber string with the white wood paddle it was attached to would be easy and it wasn't. I wheel the flimsy doll carriage without a doll on the shale driveway and the strip of cement at the back of the Kerhonkson house, wishing not for a doll but, to facilitate imagination, a long cement street like the easy Brooklyn sidewalks mothers wheel real babies on.

Queen for a Day

The Emerson TV, sent from Brooklyn to California because I'd complained to my parents of boredom, is what kept me sane. A sweet, generous, slightly dowdy woman with 2 or 3 kids drove me to Faculty Wives. I met Alice, also pregnant, at Faculty Wives. She had a little boy, born after many miscarriages, and lived in the foothills, 30 minutes from the cottage next to Bayshore we rented from Mr. Bini. With Catholic schoolgirls and pregnant women huge and jovial I rode the bus downtown, always worried something was wrong with the baby, not big enough under smocks over clever skirts and pants with cutouts in the front. Fall and winter evenings my husband and I watched comedy and drama on the Emerson and in the spring, starting with the flowering false spring I would learn came too soon every year, I watched Queen for a Day. Lured by the idea of my own washer and dryer (our house came with a washer and I hung clothes on a line in the tiny garden) I wrote a letter saying why I deserved to be Queen for a Day, manipulating the prose to convey the right amount of emotion. I understood the tears and shrieks from the queens at first glimpse of their compensatory loot: refrigerators, oversized TVs, bedroom and living room suites, freezers, matched luggage, sets of dishes, golf clubs, linens, a wardrobe from the thick mail order catalog— goods I would have sniffed at the previous year, first in line to hear T.S. Eliot. In the labor room across the hall a terrified woman about to have a Caesarean was screaming. The doctors kept coming into mine to listen, futilely, for a heartbeat. Waiting for the birth, we made plans to buy a car, go East, I would get pregnant again right away, but in Elko, Nevada, on the return trip in the aqua Chevy, its windshield forever studded with insects, I came down with intestinal flu and was out of sorts all fall. To keep my mind off conceiving, I worked for Welfare, filling out forms, interviewing elderly clients in musty houses my husband drove me to. It was not yet light the mornings I woke to get ready for the job where I was no one's friend. The night my imagination came true, my husband, resistant to prescience, especially if tragic, was teaching at an army base hours from home. I phoned Alice, whose baby girl was a month old, and she sent her husband George. Why am I writing this now—after the first days I never cried again for the stillborn boy. Bygone grief belongs in prose.

Saint Joan and Others

———
———
———
———
———

Saint Joan

The library moved over a Chinese restaurant. Then it didn't seem like a library. There was the odor of Chinese food and the library with a linoleum floor was one large room of books. I don't know why I didn't return *Saint Joan* to the Brooklyn Public Library, Kings Highway Branch, but I didn't. I still have it. *Saint Joan*. Shaw, George Bernard. The Kings Highway Branch of the library over the Chinese restaurant was not like the Prospect Park Main Branch or the 42nd Street Library Main Branch with the two placid lions, one on either side of a lip of steps. It was a room with books over a Chinese restaurant and I still have the *Saint Joan* I borrowed the last year of high school. The library moved closer to Ocean Parkway. You opened the door and climbed a long flight of stairs. Downstairs was the Chinese restaurant. I don't know why I didn't return *Saint Joan* to the library. The summer I borrowed *Escape from Freedom* for summer camp, it got returned. Although the floor was cool, in summer the room was stifling and the smell from the downstairs Chinese restaurant dampened my adolescent appetite, but it revived as I walked the long walk home, my arms with books. I took the subway to the 42nd Street Library, a seated lion on either side of the entrance of steps. While my father wrote at a table in the reading room, I read in the children's room fairy tales and *Five Little Peppers*. The library moved over a Chinese restaurant. It became a room with books over a restaurant, cool linoleum, the odor of food. I don't know why I didn't return *Saint Joan* to the Brooklyn Public Library, Kings Highway Branch. I still have it. *Saint Joan*. George Bernard Shaw. The library didn't resemble the library at Prospect Park with its turnstile like the zoo and the Botanical Gardens, or the 42nd Street Branch, protected by those lions. It was a room over a restaurant and I still have the green library *Saint Joan* I borrowed the last year of high school.

My Father's Half Brother Abe's Mother

I ask Sarah, manicuring my nails, how she feels about being so far from home. She replies, eyes down, that she misses her family in Korea. Do you and your husband speak Korean and how long has it been since you saw Korea, I ask, measuring Sarah's sadness as she puts a pale polish called linen on my nails. My life in beauty parlors—should I get my eyebrows shaped: I speak to Shelley about my fear of the process, don't reveal her name is my brother's. And optical shops: the friendly optician Marlene, who has numerous interesting tattoos and a 3-year-old daughter, can't seem to straighten my new glasses; finally she raises the right side sufficiently to match the left with its lens, thick as a wrist, then hours later it's again too low. Last night I tried to hear what the young couple and the determined woman in her forties were saying while I ate my vegetable burger and cold, mealy potatoes. She could have been a lawyer or immigration specialist, they could have been filing for divorce, from each other or he from another, some foolish mistake, to marry the silent smiling woman with the same long glossy hair as Maria, my daughter's best friend, whose funeral mass my husband came home for but then he left again, unpersuaded. I miss New York. Nostalgia doesn't help art although loss can if you don't mention it. My mother is concerned about her sister's illness but won't say what it is. My cousin died of a disease I had to pull from her word by word like a child from a well. She isn't dependent on me, she's dependent on the cleaning woman—her girl—or the Cuban woman who comes to her apartment to manicure her nails for $5. There's Abe, my father's half brother from his father's first marriage in Galicia. His father left Abe's mother behind when he came to America, or she could have been dead, a secret buried with my grandfather, a translator of holy texts, and my father, an everyday grammarian.

Mother Teresa

What I remember is that I was running not from an unknown enemy but from Adolf Hitler himself. I have material to write except when I'm at my desk and want to write. I noticed the white sweater with balls (I think they're called popcorn) the young woman at *Immortal Beloved* was wearing. Her husband (she had a sparkly band on her wedding ring finger) said he'd go get hot dogs or they'd have to eat later and came back with a tub (perhaps 2, I'm not sure) of popcorn. She kept blowing her nose at the end of *Immortal Beloved* when, after the premier performance of the 9th, deaf Beethoven, usually maligned by the Viennese, is given a huge ovation, including by "Immortal Beloved," the widow of his brother, now dead of ugly consumption (there's a dreadful scene when the brother and Ludwig fight and a thick stream of dark blood flows from the brother's mouth). I remembered "Immortal Beloved" from my opposite sex poems in Kathleen's class. Joyce says the pain in my eyes is "dry eye." She'll probably attend a writing conference in Ireland this summer; I probably won't. The rain isn't streaming down my window so Candido probably fixed the drainpipe. There is an empty space I fill, unconfident, hoping the right words will pile up. "Azygous" means unpaired—I fell and have a large painful wound devoid of skin. The collage Jan made for my birthday she framed in blue. The background is green; I'm in the center, a young Mother Teresa in white with red splotches on my cheeks (rouge or embarrassment). There's an eye and a butterfly, an unworked crossword puzzle, a quote from Christopher Morley about madness, actually 2 butterflies, a shoe with a strap and buckle, a Rebecca of Sunnybrook Farm postage stamp, actually 2, 2 legs in stockings, a jar she's labelled "The Mason Jar," etc.

Video Clerk with No Hand

When my friend asks for money I say I'll help her out but she isn't at the café where I drive in the pounding rain. The ringing phone is my friend. She fell asleep. It's raining so hard could I drive from the café to her place. When I get there she's waiting on the porch, drying her hair, wet from the walk to and from the phone booth in the rain, by now tropical. Her eye makeup is running. I may have ruined my black boots walking to her porch. The young video store clerk has no hand; where a hand should have been is a red, thin, burned-looking end, an instrument, a pipe or a stick. I do not want to stare. I want to ignore her no hand. I delay so as not to seem curious or repelled, take my time completing the transaction, joke a bit. At the pizza place we are eating salad, not yet pizza, at a small table in the middle close to the door when I see two people vacate a booth against the wall away from the door. I take my salad and tell my spouse we should move there. The woman who works at the pizza place and closely resembles the woman who used to work there and once asked what I was reading is right now standing at the booth and could clean it with her spray and cloth. Therefore I don't put my salad down. But my spouse puts his down and transfers our glasses, cutlery and napkins so she thinks people are still eating there and moves away. I tell him the other people's germs must be washed off before I eat there. He says people are waiting, we should sit down at the new booth, move firmly away from the old table I'm standing at with my salad in my hand. I turn to the couple I hadn't noticed in back of us, waiting, not impatiently, but waiting, and remain standing at the old table, salad in hand, until the booth has been cleaned. In the theatre there are separate wheel-chair sections at the back. If people in wheelchairs can't hear or see so far from the stage, in a slightly raised section like a prisoners' cage, they have to put up with it. During intermission a man standing against the side wall close to the stage, his eyes closed, breathes very slowly and noisily. At lunch, at the counter, an attractive young couple, maybe tourists from New York, maybe newlyweds on their honeymoon trip, spoke as if they hadn't known each other long but long enough to be comfortable. She had hot dogs and beans—he had one hot dog on rye bread, a hot dog sandwich. Both had curly hair and wore anoraks; she carried a plastic bag printed Crown Books.

Jewish Shakespeare

Back from their honeymoon they visit my mother's sister Sadie, whose husband I think commits suicide. They bring Sadie a beaded purse, her boys lollipops. Sadie sloshes eggs and milk for French toast, I remember having French toast for the first time at Aunt Sadie's, when we brought my cousin the small pocketbook I wanted, why I buy so many pocketbooks now. My cousin is from the next marriage—in this marriage Sadie gives perms and colors hair in the bedroom, at night makes lampshades. Her husband, soon a suicide, I'm pretty sure a suicide, sells dry goods, thread, buttons, pins door-to-door five days a week. Already my mother has dark circles like old blood under the eyes and my father, still studying literature, is called Shakespeare by her cackling unmarried sisters and hunchback brother. For her, lacy blouses and long brown hair loosely twisted in a bun, Shakespeare will give up literature, will make their children's lives miserable and safe, will fill their conventional apartment with biographies, Jewish stories in English, *Alice in Wonderland,* poetry, a book where animals are people though they hibernate like animals— this hibernating excites me, I cannot get this hibernating out of my mind. In the kitchen of my aunt and the suicide, who is not the father of the cousin we brought the pocketbook I wanted, newlywed Shakespeare, I imagine, thinks of his mother, dead of TB, whom he nursed while his father was translating the Pentateuch into Hebrew and Yiddish and running errands for my father's brother and half brother, jewelers.

Hilda Doolittle and Other Modern American Poets

Elise and I walked back and forth across the street from Mrs. Vanderpool's house. Dorothy Vanderpool. Married to a Navy man, an officer, at sea more than home. Mrs. V's eyes were blue. She wore suits and pale silky blouses with collars. And clunky laced shoes. She was as tall as Judy Reisner, whom I was taller than. Boys and girls lined up in two unsegregated columns at the sides of the classroom, each column taking turns walking to her front-center desk. We had narrowed the possibilities: her house must be that one and we stalked it, hoping she would go in or come out. I remember her coming out once to walk her dog. Elise and I lived ten blocks away from the neighborhood of private homes owned by gentiles, Elise's apartment house one block from mine, across the street, Ocean Avenue, that used to have trolley tracks. What did I expect. That seeing me, us, she would evidence pleasure. No. The most I expected was to glimpse her in the plain world we occupied separately, where, briefly, she might not be the woman of principle, sometimes cruel, like when she made Lenny confess he didn't have a father, and I wouldn't be the pathetic child with holes in her socks. Every morning after the flag salute we recited poems we'd memorized. I recited Hilda Doolittle, Sara Teasdale, Edwin Markham, Emily Dickinson, Robinson Jeffers, Walt Whitman, Edna St. Vincent Millay. Mr. Vanderpool, a large man, travelled, and Mrs. Vanderpool was childless. I flushed at her compliment for my red sweater, the first new clothing that year. My mother bought it on the Lower East Side while I had my piano lesson at the Eighth Street Settlement. I played one piece, a Mozart sonata, until my teacher decided we'd both done all we could and I should play it for Miss Valentine, who had called my brother talented. I played miserably, of course, and quit the Eighth Street Settlement to take private lessons with Mrs. Moskowitz, who came to the house and taught me

"Malagueña." There is a relationship between language and memory. The day my brother was accepted at Harvard, I blurted it out to Mrs. V from my desk, in front of hers so she could keep an eye on me. "Wonderful," she said, or even "Class, listen to Phyllis's remarkable news," and then, whether or not she said this, I imagine her piercing my brown eyes with the cold blue of hers and asking "What will you do with *your* life?" The rhythms of prose are the rhythms of life. I married a man who wanted to be gone and left, came back and left again. She never touched me, not my shoulder, my hand, my hair. She led me to the teachers' room on the first day of my second menstrual period. I had thrown up and didn't tell her why.

Tristan

Although his partner had recently died of AIDS, he was OK, the hairdresser with the name of a rock star, not feeling well, coughing softly occasionally, not joining in the conversation much, but eating a lot and with appetite. Tell me he's not HIV positive—listen, whether or not he is, I am beginning to understand that all gay men, even gay men totally safe, fear it, hysterically, every illness, every scratch. Do I, straight, have the right to say this. The yellow trees, the same yellow as other years, this year thrill me. Murder, murder, murder—I keep saying no more movies with murder but there's nothing else. The years of preparing for death are many. Perhaps my watch is losing time. The watch man said on the 30th he was changing it to the 31st so it would become the 1st tomorrow but today it became the 1st and it's the 2nd. I should breathe like a swimmer, though I don't swim, not blending unduly, not stuck-up, just not blending unduly—what I mean by not blending unduly: retaining outlines. A pretty woman theorizes about good and evil, married to a man almost as quiet as the hairdresser and with a slight tic, and she seems happy though she talks too fast and a bit compulsively with somewhat too much humor. I also theorize about good and evil, talking too fast a bit compulsively. We all laugh, pretty cheerful for the moment, retaining outlines, say a paper doll with tabs and white cotton underwear, Jane Withers or Judy Garland, unmarried so OK to be seen in underwear. After dinner, like last year, minus the hairdresser's partner, we walk to the peacocks in the tree, which I, only I, at first can't locate, then to the new houses, brick and wood—on the other side, low down, the freeway—you hear it and you don't—I respectfully step back, despite the berth of long-established houses between me and the huge drop. Forty years after we made love in his furnished basement, he returns, drives me to that Brooklyn house he finds easily, reminds me that night he played Richard Wagner's *Tristan*. Oh his name is Richard. What did we know.

Miss Kramer

Barbara Schwartz was never my friend but she grew to tolerate me, even, I thought, to like me, though I always got the vocabulary right in Miss Kramer's French class and was the Dean's daughter. I didn't envy her body, I envied her huge lipsticked lips. I couldn't wear lipstick. Dean's rule. I didn't go to the Dean's wife, my mother, and plead with her to ask the Dean to let me wear lipstick, at least to the freshman dance. I didn't dance. I didn't dance at the first college dance, a jolly-up, either. So many men, a hot noisy room filled with men, and no one asked me to dance. A woman in her twenties in a Polish film goes to bed with the first man who ever asked her to dance. She'll poison him. She'll also poison a man who asks her to dance the night she'd poisoned the first man who asked her to dance. And she'll poison her father, who kicked her out of the house when she was pregnant, and she'll poison her mother. Her mother picked the chicken or meat (maybe a dumpling) out of her daughter's soup. Her mother ate the chicken, meat or dumpling with satisfaction. The daughter said nothing.

Hemingway

Mrs. Skillsky once worked at a cash register beside her teen-aged son, only to see the boy offered training opportunities that she was denied.
—The New York Times, *December 17, 1993*

The writer is trying to write but the mother keeps having unmotherly thoughts. What can a mother write about envying her son that will not alienate readers, including her son. Overhead planes are making a terrible racket, like bombers in a forties' movie. Easier to focus on bombers than the envy eating away her desire to write. Is that why she stopped writing in college, because she couldn't compete with the rivals around the workshop table. And now her son is one of them. This dark foggy morning in January, the indefinite month she hates, though she knows competition, even the subject, is a waste, she realizes it must be written about, written about and written about. Even writing that is difficult. Maybe her son envies his mother, a woman. And why does he tell her mother, not his, about his new book, an opportunity for her mother to tell her what she should feel. She would like to feel that easy mother pride in a brilliant son instead of this degrading pessimism about her own work. She dreamed her friend received a phone call from her lover and ran from the motel shower. She hasn't been that enamoured since college but she doesn't envy her friend, she envies her son, who was in high school when she began writing again. And if he competes with his mother, it doesn't stop his cocky, funny memories, the bright flow which reminds her, yes it does, of hers. She thinks of the tableau in the living room, the room with the fire escape facing the empty lot. Her father has asked Mr. Sher, her brother's piano teacher, to listen to her sing. Mr. Sher finds her voice ordinary. Her brother is the musical child. Her "Für Elise," years later the Mozart sonata with its many difficult movements, is ignored. This envy shames her. It brings back the summer at Flotz's, the undistinguished hotel in the Adirondacks where they were the only Jews and middle-aged couples and spinster teachers in white cottons whiled away hours on the motion picture lawn. She chewed gum like mad, increasing its volume with gum wrapper foil and scraps from her father's notebooks, her mother's *Redbook* and *Ladies' Home Journal.* Her brother was at his out-of-town college escaping the war. There was no one young to talk to and dreary days were punctuated only by the three enormous meals of pale, unfamiliar German food: potatoes cooked myriad ways, sliced fatty meats, creamed vegetables. She walked and read, ate, read and walked. What book was she reading that summer. A long one but not *Jean Christophe,* perhaps *The Fountainhead,* or a Hemingway—had *For Whom the Bell Tolls* been published. She didn't envy her brother then. He had led the way out.

Eunice

Phil and Martha, my husband and I, drove to Amherst in our '34 (or '35) black Pontiac to look it over since Phil might go to school there. The window on the passenger side had cardboard instead of glass, though I think that was later. The sun came out in the afternoon—it was spring. We had thought not to go because of the occasional light rain, which was why we ate our little picnic—cold cut sandwiches, chips, fruit and cookies—in the Pontiac. Uneven, but not one of the streaked sky days I love, a day when the sky has white childish penmanship, the handwriting of badly behaved men and surprisingly emotional women. There may be red surrounding. Orangey red of pastels I always thought I'd like to try my hand at. Days before rain, days of almost rain, days of rain beginning, rain you can see through, not the swollen rain in Iowa 3 years later, driving across country after the stillbirth. Nothing was set. Good things could happen. Not just the money the men with advanced degrees would earn, that would mean for Martha and Phil no more horse meat that tasted like horse meat no matter how it was cooked. Eunice, a bride like me, pranced around the next-door apartment, shrieking as her husband (they were Australian) chased her, slapping his prize, her ample buttocks. Pleasure, that was what could happen.

Blond Moviegoer

In the movie café, early for *Falling Down,* he reads news, I read book reviews and stare at a blond whose hair is probably dyed. I move from her to a man and a woman walking together into the theatre. Where have I seen them before. He's wearing a camel's-hair jacket and she's dressed up for an event, surely not the movies, maybe an event they've come from. They both have prominent sparkling eyeglasses and I see them as churchgoers as they separate for Men and Women. I listen to the blond's voice before I try to hear her words. Does her voice have anything to do with her hair. My youngest son sometimes hints he has no solution but one. Why does my daughter still blame me. The blond asks her boyfriend or husband, wearing jeans and black leather jacket, if cemetery has an "A," like *Pet Sematary,* and he tells her correctly no "A," maybe you're thinking of seminary. I compare my mind and the mind of a writer whose book is reviewed and grieve, not for any specific loss, for death, for having to accept what I have as adequate. The blond and her mate or date at 12 midnight walk out from *Falling Down,* not *Pet Sematary,* before me and my mate. She's wearing a black leather jacket over her blouse and the upper part of her black tights. She's thin, shapely. I haven't exercised for days. Now at my desk before breakfast, I hear the distant sighing of birds or animals and the off-and-on flow of cars, trucks and buses from the expressway, traffic which probably never stops though I hear it continuously off and on, off and on.

Joyce

Sam, my first boyfriend, a Joyce scholar, lives in Boston and after 40 years contacted me in California 5 years ago, married at the time to Samantha, his 3rd wife. Two years ago Sam met Cindy, his 4th wife, but didn't tell me, instead said now I could leave messages on his answering machine because he'd told Samantha about us, although, as I would learn, Samantha, a classicist, was no longer living in his house on weekends, their marital arrangement, Cindy, whom he hadn't married yet, was, not every weekend since she teaches English in Michigan. There is a MacDougal Street restaurant with dripping candles where Sam insists he tried to convince me 40 years ago, after a cab ride, to take him back. I didn't take a cab to Sam's daughter's loft in the Village, my husband drove me. There Sam fainted in the tiny bathroom and for all I knew he could have been dead or was going to die. In the conversation where, 2 years after the fact, he finally told me about Cindy, his prospective bride, prompted by my finally commenting on the cooling of our phone calls and occasional meetings, Sam said the Village loft sex that went nowhere was not behind his belief we never would have an affair, my turning down his invitation to spend a week in London was, although when he invited me to London he explicitly said that didn't mean sex, and that belief, depressing to him, as he said I should understand, led to sex in London with Cindy, sex which he felt he deserved. Sex: Latin, *sexus,* perhaps akin to *secare,* to divide. Incidentally, he told me prior to the events he never admitted were humiliating, when I was walking around the loft viewing the flashy inexpert art of the painter his daughter had sublet from, the untruth he claims at the time he considered truth that he'd never leave Samantha. Sam, a fictional name, referred me to the diamond salesman with a sexual name, Balz, who sold my mother's huge diamond for $1/3$ its value. In the conversation in which he confessed about Cindy, after I'd accused him of being a bad friend, he cited the referral as an act of friendship, just before he hung up abruptly, in too much pain from finally confessing to continue. I've wanted my mother to know Sam and I are in touch again, have wanted her to reflect gloomily, i.e., guiltily, on the past, but I only tell her I understand Sam has married for the 4th time. She responds, probably in a dream, by reminding me of the trouble I've caused her, I assume work, worry, etc. since she doesn't know I sold the diamond she gave me early to preclude wrangling between my brother and me after she dies, wrangling which could complete the 40-year-old breach in existence since the psychoanalyst-to-be interpreted Sam's behaviour to our mother and eager father as alarming symptoms and they manipulated our breakup. Next she asks how many years of Latin I had in high school, a non sequitur, yet not illogical, especially in a dream. I take the offensive, answering loudly, "Only 2, Mother, and now I wish it had been 4." I don't say 3, like my brother, 1 more than my 2, I say 4, 1 more than his 3. I can feel the ire rising. I go on—"Mother, a poet needs to know the roots of words."

Unavenging Japanese Father

In Japan a father travels by railroad with his weeping wife to families of crime victims to do something, but not vengeance, for the son who died in his arms begging him to avenge his death. At first he wanted only the death of the murderer who killed his son only because his son happened to be the one passing by. Everything is wrong in my family and my life. From the avenue of the shopping center comes the sound of an ambulance or fire engine as in a movie from England, the sound I didn't think our emergency vehicles made. I ask my children's father if he would mind sleeping downstairs. He doesn't mind. It's like a movie. I turn on the light to write it down. I must stop thinking how this reads. I must say what must be said, and already I've changed it. I deceive myself with changes. That's been changed. If I dream, the dream will be to the siren what the siren was to the TV movie. The words accumulate. Some words have to be changed.

Terese

I found out I had high blood pressure at a neighborhood walk-in clinic the night I got stung by yellow jackets. It was the night of Terese's divorce class at Kaiser—I heard Terese has cancer. I'd gone out to water the purple agapanthus at the side of the house with the eucalyptus, that fast-growing tree whose trunk peels like sunburned skin. Arcadio, who called himself Art and rode a motorcycle, had given me a perm that afternoon. He and Arno owned their own salon on Winchester. Arno had a German accent and lisped. I guess the scent of that goo they use for perms attracted the bees, propelling me, screaming like a hurt block kid, to Rose's. Terese's class met Wednesdays so Rose would have been sitting at the kitchen counter marking the food specials. The block and the night I got stung enter my mind after the fireman leads the woman having a breakdown out of the coffeehouse where I'm reading and sipping a cappuccino. One bad thing then another took Rose by surprise around the time her mother finally let the doctors cut off her hand, too late, like in my mother's lending library novels. What Rose and I had in common were our four children, the housework to maintain our serious tract houses, our obsession with disease. After the stillbirth I was afraid of heart disease, cancer of the uterus, cancer of the cervix, leukemia. It's possible I began to be afraid of dying that year of daily humiliation, the year I got my period. Just before or after, my grandmother had a stroke while I was at school. I saw the ambulance as I rounded the corner and knew she'd had another, as I'd feared, in my house, and when my mother said you know what that is I realized I did know that what we'd been warned in Hygiene happened to girls with bodies like mine had happened to me.

Vietnam Son

Ms. Orchid and I gave a reading at the Y when she was married to a poet disinclined to ambition. The husband she married next died (I meet her occasionally at the window of the government agency where she works) and she has dyed her hair—I mean a totally different color. I wasn't writing yet. In the back seat of a car like an Oldsmobile my ambitious husband and I were going with our former neighbors Sarge and Willie to visit their son on drugs and the wife he'd met in Sweden dodging the draft. Movies had explicit sex, ordinary movies, and we had started seeing them. I was thinking about the movies in the back seat, feeling superior because I couldn't imagine a son of mine going off the deep end like Willie's and because I believed Sarge and Willie no longer had sex. Sarge, who'd been a sergeant in the Second World War, was a none-too-successful car salesman. His wife Willie, for years my best friend, in addition to painting large abstracts that looked like art but you couldn't live with them, typed for college professors, including my husband, who got up at 4 a.m. to write his books in the garage. Sarge and Willie's other son, their son's friend, adopted when he was in high school and kicked out of his foster home (the things you remember), Tom or George, he had an ordinary name, went to Vietnam and shortly after his welcome home party in the park near Sarge and Willie's apartment killed himself. Willie after all that time got pregnant and they moved to a new house in a suburb so remote it could be another city. Orchid is not her name—she's actually given herself the name of a tree. I wore pleated skirts in elementary school and during Vietnam the skirt of my red knit suit was pleated. Not only 2 famous men writers died this month, a woman 15 years my senior, famous enough to have a *New York Times* obituary, died. Lately I've been dreaming about the Brooklyn apartment I lived in until I went away to college—I can't move out of that apartment, I mean I am repeatedly literally in the process of moving out.

Juliet

A young Sharon looks like someone else's daughter, the same unreflective round face. Her hair is permed, not unbecomingly—no more bouffant, no more cigarettes. I expect her to have acne but she doesn't. Who is she. The Charon who ferries souls to Hell is a man. And which river. Lethe's drinkers forget their past, Sharon reminds me of it— whenever I want most to forget, I am most reminded. Her black suit is history, its jacket worn to *Romeo & Juliet,* its skirt brought to the consignment shop because, like her, I have gained weight. Or is it the river Styx, not Lethe, as in sticks and stones will break my bones. You suck me dry, my words over a late dinner at the downtown restaurant I raise my voice to men in. Sharon's daughter didn't marry early like Sharon, she's living with her boyfriend, and I understand she's gotten really large, as large as the neighbor who bakes, who's in a wheelchair, whom I should visit. My thin daughter, too thin to go to Weight Watchers, goes to Weight Watchers. I get on the scale in the kitchen every morning before I go downstairs to write. I take hormones and bleed like a girl.

Rembrandt

I lift my arms over my head, stretch as high as I can, and in the mirror look almost thin, look as I may have looked as a girl. I can't remember my young body. I'm sorry I didn't like it enough to memorize. So why am I not more sympathetic towards my mother, her ancient body more mine than the young girl's she once dressed. She doesn't even help me pack for Europe, hurries me along to the boat she and my father took to Europe on their honeymoon, later, to Europe again, with my aunt and barrister uncle. My uncle may not have gone to college, just law school, or not law school, just college. Forced to quit high school to work, of course my mother feels that my 4 years at my brother's elite college meant he wasn't favored. Summer days in the country there was nothing to do but read, no occasional obligatory zoo with smelly monkey house and roasted peanuts and dull Botanical Gardens with irrelevant flowers and the nearby dark museum with roped rooms of furniture, paintings of Dutch men and women and landscapes without people. In the spring we went on field trips to the Brooklyn Museum and could buy small colored prints like the savings stamps to bring our boys home: I liked the savings stamps as much as Rembrandt. Summer nights during World War II we went to every new movie playing in Ellenville, where we also borrowed library books, some weeks the same books, some years the same books. I was ashamed of my father, harsh in the presence of my friends and always asking questions. None except Leona had visible fathers and hers went on the road to Pennsylvania 5 days a week to sell clothes, men's, I think, in overcoat and hat and carrying a suitcase. He probably had a mistress in Pennsylvania—I knew about that from books and movies. We lived on the 2nd floor too, Leona in a 1-bedroom apartment across from the stairs. Leona's mother blamed me for our broken friendship, not my father, who broke it, but when I am chased up the stairs by a rapist and knock on their door, she lets me come in.

Italian Rose

My dental hygienist tells me about her affair as she probes, scrapes and polishes. I'd noticed her blush several minutes before as I commented on her sapphire earrings. I'd already noticed how well she looked, indeed had told her in the waiting room, where she was flossing her teeth as we chatted prior to my appointment, that she looked 10 years younger. She wears pink gloves and a pink mask. And the large electric toothbrush is purple, the pink and purple, reflections, I think, of her new self, although of course she had nothing to do with their selection. I tell her to think of herself, acting a part, acting as if I consider affairs all right, even telling her I came close to having an affair, acting as if it had been more than temptation. Right now I'm waiting for the sound of the lock on the front door, which will mean my husband has left for the day. Sometimes he doesn't lock the door and I remember the door the bride's husband hadn't locked, her murder not shouted across the street by the jovial rotund fundamentalist minister to my former husband leaving in his Buick for his existential philosophy class, sung like a recitative to me on my way to Italian Rose's morning coffee, next door to the newlyweds' stentorian preacher, who sometimes walked with a cane, sometimes used a wheelchair, sometimes walked unaided. My dental hygienist is as red as this pen, as red as profuse new blood. Her thick neck, lined like the neck of a much older woman, bleeds embarrassment. It stays red as she makes an anti-Semitic remark linking Jews and money, referring to the Jewish surgeon with a new kidney. Such nastiness in the past I thought harmless, considering her, like me, harmless. I want to think the threat of AIDS from her exaggerated, even hysterical, like the likelihood of pregnancy from semen spilled outside my vagina in my first, rushed, intercourse on a Brooklyn roof. The enflamed hygienist is speaking so loudly her affair can be heard by anyone passing the open door. I don't like being in the suburban neighborhood where I was a conventional mother and wife, until, under the pressure I applied, the shining disguises cracked. I want to break the conventional boundaries of art.

Stanley Elkin

A man slips on the ice on a New York street and makes the front page. Here, isolating fog: droplets of water on my slanted window. The streets of the unfamiliar town are crowded, the businesses open all night. It is late and the store, bazaar-like, like Woolworth's, has no items I want to buy and no Xerox machine. I am finally reading Stanley Elkin's vastly difficult sentences. The New Year's Eve of 1948 my boyfriend and I, brimming poets, went to a movie on 42nd Street. I see in a card on my desk 2 birds, one, in flight, beautiful and red-breasted, maybe a tanager, one, perched, less graceful, colored a sort of mottled green and yellow close to young pea pods. And in another I see a city street reminiscent of the fifties, 3 parked cars under a thin layer of recently fallen snow (it is no longer snowing). At 3 short flights of stairs leading to 3 houses there are 2 garbage cans, the first part of the stairs of the middle house curved like an arm, its 2 garbage cans in the elbow, the entire small flight twisted like important internal organs. Probably New York City. A modest neighborhood, the snow hiding squalor and beauty like stranding, liberating fog. Who knows what goes on inside these houses with front steps. Who knows who drives these cars, what jobs their drivers have. Passing by garbage cans in a city like New York sometimes you are assaulted by a strong odor: the same odor at the back of restaurants, even expensive restaurants. The houses are close together and one has curtains and shrubs barely sprinkled with snow. I wanted to cross the street away from the store attracting foolish tourists, childlike, coins jingling in their pockets, the way my father used to bounce his change, signifying time was running out, but he, the son of a poor Biblical scholar, had more money than he needed—the mere sound could weaken a child's resolve. I wanted to cross the street, exchange the just-designed ring for the more appropriate original. The ring was tall, sharp as an icicle—bind yourself, finally, to a more reckless future. I sometimes think, for a breath, that I hear nothing.

Brooklyn Ballerina

Despite the weather, the shape of my body in its pink bathrobe suggests I am beyond the smack of the telephone. It will be my daughter or my son, not likely the man that called once with his heavy breathing. My friend has never been caught in the snow before but this time she will be, she will be caught and will love it. Sweets tempt me less. But memory, which my friend says she doesn't have but remembers her dead cat, is not the problem. I couldn't help naming what I think I no longer want. The woman who grew up in an orphan asylum remembers but doesn't talk about it. The nerve of the telephone. Data tempts me less. But snow might. One child resembles another. Remember tripping to the library, hearing "Dance Ballerina Dance" from a loudspeaker piped to Kings Highway passersby, remember, though it pains to be back, imagining you liked that music, in the mood of "Dance Ballerina Dance" imagining you could stay in Brooklyn forever.

Alan Roland

Had we already decided to marry the time we took a bus a Saturday or Sunday to the North Shore, the town with streets narrow as hallways, the tiny wood houses like the dollhouse in Alan Roland's backyard. No ocean in view, no fried clams—which I loved. Everything ahead and I saw it needn't be ominous: I could study again and write papers; the two girls in the dormitory who'd tried to kill themselves, both on Sunday nights, had failed. What am I getting at. He rolled up his white shirtsleeves, something virgin Nancy Ryan found sexual, ironed patches on the seat of his black trousers. He wore the trousers and a black clip bow tie ushering for the Boston Symphony. The smell of first spring in New England that I absolutely can't smell now. And around that time, the spring before graduation and marriage, we were invited to a gathering in the town adjacent to the university—a just-married couple—he'd probably met the man at the Boylston Street restaurant where he was a short-order cook. And I could see myself engaged with the wife's cheap workaday diamond, $100 or $200 in store windows, not likely a store with diamond rings in the window in that ocean town, the ocean not visible. I keep coming back to this kind of writing, unambitious prose from easy, unimportant memory. The men drink beer, men and women smoke. He's next to me on the couch, I'm wearing a dark blue sophisticated dress with deep V-neck, full faille skirt, blue kid pumps, false pearls, pearl earrings. Not the car he sometimes borrowed from the man I was afraid of, a steady at the restaurant, a bus to the ocean, where the ocean wasn't visible, where that day what I thought I wanted was visible; but then I studied for exams and it was totally satisfying studying in Widener, though when I first began to study, after the year I couldn't, I could only study in a city library, as if I were in high school again or going to college, living at home, as my mother would have liked. I never wanted what I couldn't have, a pretty classmate's marriage, her graduate school in education, job in an affluent suburb, and accepted what I absolutely could not picture—but weren't there doubts, admit you had doubts. I started studying—admit you loved studying—and when by doing what was absolutely necessary, no excessive ambition, I passed, I adapted to that smaller role, except sometimes—admit it— the old hunger pushed the sentences, rather in between, as you hope it does in this kind of writing.

Birthday Girl

This happens a lot in restaurants. At the sushi bar, to my right, there are two men and a girl between them. The girl says she wants two scoops of ice cream: red bean and green tea. It's her birthday. The server says you can't order two scoops, only one scoop, so the girl says OK, then she'll have one scoop and one scoop. And indeed the server brings her one scoop in one dish and one scoop in another dish, two scoops, both of green tea because they're out of red bean. This is quite funny but not a joke. The birthday girl (and the chef calls her birthday girl—everything the chef says he says smiling) has amazing lips: how can I describe them. She could be an actress in a movie with those lips but I don't think she is an actress in a movie, with the two fellows, one on each side, ordering sushi as if it were free, until the two scoops in two dishes come, then only the two order and then the check comes, which my neighbor, hunched towards the lips girl, like my son sitting on his foot at my kitchen table and hunched towards me, puts down a single hundred for and the other fellow, hunched like the other fellow towards the girl with lips, for his half tosses a card. Some years ago I wrote a poem about people in a movie theatre in San Francisco's Japantown eating noodles from styrofoam cups, a poem I never completed: no matter what form I put it in I couldn't complete it. To my left there is a young woman with the smallest wrists imaginable. A man old enough to be the chef's father, carrying a wooden boat, sits down at the other end of the emptying bar. The chef almost stops smiling, almost beads with sweat (from time to time, between sushi preparations, he wipes his face with the side of a hand, then wipes the hand on his white chef trousers). The boat man wears glasses. I've never seen a sushi chef with glasses but why shouldn't a sushi chef like a surgeon wear glasses. How respectfully, though rapidly, the chef slices the fish he's slicing, almost as if he's slicing himself. "Thank you," "Thank you," he and I say as I leave, one *Thank you* each. In the poem I didn't complete, my movie neighbor and his, who knew each other outside the movie, said: "How **are** you," "How **are** you," one *How are you* each.